stir-fries

stir-fries

hamlyn

First published in Great Britain in 2002 by
Hamlyn, a division of
Octopus Publishing Group Limited
2–4 Heron Quays, London E14 4JP

Copyright © 2002
Octopus Publishing Group Limited

Reprinted 2003

ISBN 0 600 60705 4

Printed in China

Notes

1 Standard level spoon measurements are used in all recipes.

2 Measurements for canned food have been given as a standard imperial equivalent.

3 Eggs should be large unless otherwise stated. The FDA advises that eggs should not be consumed raw. This book may contain dishes made with lightly cooked eggs. It is prudent for more vulnerable people, such as pregnant and nursing mothers, invalids, the elderly, babies, and young children, to avoid uncooked or lightly cooked dishes made with eggs. Once prepared, these dishes should be used immediately.

4 Poultry should be cooked thoroughly. To test if poultry is cooked, pierce the flesh through the thickest part with a skewer or fork—the juices should run clear, never pink or red.

5 Use whole milk unless otherwise stated.

6 Fresh herbs should be used unless otherwise stated. If unavailable, use dried herbs as an alternative but halve the quantities stated.

7 Pepper should be freshly ground black pepper unless otherwise stated; season according to taste.

8 Ovens should be preheated to the specified temperature—if using a convection oven, follow the manufacturer's instructions for adjusting the time and the temperature.

9 Do not re-freeze a dish that has been frozen previously.

10 This book includes dishes made with nuts and nut derivatives. It is advisable for people with known allergic reactions to nuts and nut derivatives and those who may be potentially vulnerable to these allergies, such as pregnant and nursing mothers, invalids, the elderly, babies, and children, to avoid dishes made with nuts and nut oils.
It is also prudent to check the labels of prepared ingredients for the possible inclusion of nut derivatives.

Surprisingly filling, rice and noodle based dishes excel as main courses or special side dishes. Try the tantalizing Coconut Rice with Fish and Peas on its own and serve Spicy Fried Rice with one of the meat dishes.

Combining two of the most popular trends in cooking—fast and healthy—these fresh and delicious dishes will be a hit with family and friends as a main course or accompaniment.

Extremely versatile and good for you, fish is a superb main ingredient for weekday meals for the family and stylish entertaining alike.

Feel like chicken, turkey, or duck tonight? Try one of these yummy recipes such as Ginger Chicken with Honey or Sesame Marinated Turkey and get your tastebuds dancing!

From the tangy Sweet & Sour Pork to the hot and spicy Szechuan Dry-fried Shredded Beef these fabulous and hearty dishes can be whipped up any-time of the year with great success.

contents

6

introduction

Stir-frying is one of the simplest and healthiest of cooking methods. Speed is its real advantage, turning ingredients into an exciting dish in minutes while preserving their excellent food value. The technique usually brings to mind the wok and Chinese food, in particular, but its use is far more widespread. A fabulous variety of Southeast Asian dishes are stir-fried to perfection.

The Western equivalent, sautéing, is a similar method of cooking over high heat in a large pan (the classic sauté pan is slightly deeper than the usual frying pan), tossing and turning the food vigorously. Generous lumps of lard or butter are traditional for sautéing, which does not have a reputation for being healthy and is now usually replaced by stir-frying. Modern cooks have transformed oriental stir-frying into a versatile international technique for ingredients and seasonings as diverse as their countries of origin.

Equipment
A wok is the traditional pan for stir-frying, and there are many different types of woks available in stores today. Some are sold as complete sets with chopsticks, lids, and various accessories.

Woks and Pans
A wok is not essential, but you will need a large pan to allow plenty of room for combining the ingredients (many stir-fries are one-pot meals) without having them flying over the top as you stir and cook.

Woks The traditional carbon steel wok is designed for cooking over an open brazier —its thin metal dome sits neatly in a frame over a fierce outdoor fire or gas burner and conducts heat well, so it heats rapidly and the heat spreads out well. A wide top and deep sloping sides are ideal for shaking, tossing, and turning ingredients, ensuring they fall back into the bottom, rather than out over the top. Used daily, cleaned with fresh oil and paper (with salt for scouring the metal), carbon steel is fine, but if it is not in frequent use and washed without being seasoned (heated with oil) it rusts. There is a good choice of woks that can be washed and stored without oiling, some with slightly flatter bases for optimum cooking on the average gas or electric stove. Look for a wok with a domed, close-fitting lid, which is useful for retaining moisture when simmering (often used briefly after stir-frying to complete the cooking) or for steaming food placed on a rack in the wok.

Frying pans A large frying pan with fairly deep sides can be used. A classic sauté pan designed to withstand high temperatures and with deep, straight sides is ideal. A large skillet—a deep, straight-sided and covered frying pan—can be more practical than some woks since its flat base heats quickly and evenly and the deep sides allow plenty of room for tossing ingredients.

Saucepans A large saucepan is practical if it has a wide base that conducts heat well and withstands high temperatures without burning. Do not be tempted to cook

"I feel a recipe is only a theme, which an intelligent
cook can play each time with a variation."

Madame Benoit

large amounts in a small or medium saucepan as the ingredients will not be in contact with the bottom and they will not fry sufficiently quickly.

Stainless steel A good-quality stainless steel wok or pan with a base manufactured to conduct heat well can be used over high heat and the sides will also become hot. Follow the manufacturer's instructions for years of excellent use from this type of wok or pan.

Nonstick finishes These can be problematic as many nonstick surfaces do not respond well to being heated empty and they do not last well when used over high heat. Nonstick woks do conduct heat properly, but stir-frying is often carried out over a high heat and this reduces the life of the coating. Metal utensils are not suitable, but there are plenty of alternatives that won't damage the wok.

8

Oils and Fats

Stir-frying is done rapidly, therefore ingredients require minimum cooking and must withstand the vigorous stirring. Firm fish and shellfish; lean and tender cuts of meat; chicken, turkey, and duck breast (without fat); and all sorts of vegetables and fruit are ideal. Cooked rice and noodles can also be stir-fried briefly. All ingredients should be in prime condition as quick cooking emphasizes any shortfall in quality. **Basic vegetable oil** is versatile and suitable for most ingredients; peanut oil withstands high heat and is ideal for rapidly browning and crisping strips of poultry or meat; olive oil does not withstand high temperatures, but it can be used for briefly stir-frying over less fierce heat.

Sesame oil is popular in oriental dishes, but overheats rapidly and is rarely used as the main oil in which to cook food, but is more often added as a flavoring. It can be combined with vegetable oil for frying or added toward the end of cooking.
Butter is not used in oriental cooking, but is good with vegetables and other ingredients in Western-style dishes. Ideally, it should be clarified (melted and cooked gently until its water content has evaporated, then strained to remove any milk solids) so that it can be heated to a high temperature without burning. A little butter with olive oil is a well-balanced option.
Lard is a classic fat for oriental as well as Western dishes and can be heated to a high temperature. However, it is no longer popular for everyday cooking. If it is not hot enough, lard will give a greasy result.

Preparation
All ingredients must be prepared or assembled before starting to stir-fry. Minutes spent finding seasoning or spices in the middle of stir-frying can result in ingredients that overcook, becoming juicy and soft rather than retaining a crisp, fresh texture. Everything should be cut into pieces that cook quickly and evenly. Thin slices, fine strips, small cubes, and dice are typical. Tender foods that cook very fast (and may overcook) can be cut into slightly thicker slices, larger chunks, or fingers, especially when combined with firm ingredients.

The Technique
Before adding any ingredients, the oil must be hot. Depending on its type, the pan can be heated empty until very hot before adding oil. This is useful for meat as the combination of a very hot pan and oil seals the pieces fast before they release any juices that can spoil the stir-frying. For most dishes, it is usually best to heat the oil in the pan, starting over a moderate heat so that the pan can heat thoroughly.
Adding ingredients The food is rarely cooked together in one batch. Ingredients that require the longest cooking time are stir-fried first, until partly cooked, then they are pushed to one side of the pan as the remaining food is added in stages according to how long it takes to cook. Ingredients can also be stir-fried, then removed from the pan to be returned when the remainder of the dish has been assembled.
Stirring and turning Simply stirring ingredients around is not enough: the food should be moved from the edge of the pan towards the middle using a turning and stirring motion. This ensures that all the pieces are evenly cooked on all sides.
Serving Stir-fried dishes are often served freshly cooked. Have bowls or serving dishes warmed and make sure everyone is ready to eat before you begin cooking. Many one-pot meals can be served straight from the pan (if it is nice enough), especially a wok as the narrow base will fit over a candle warmer and the wide top allows plenty of space for serving the food at the table.

oodles of rice & noodles

12

spicy fried rice with red chilies

1 Rinse the rice in a sieve under cold running water and drain well. Place the rice in a saucepan, pour in the water, and add salt to taste. Bring to a boil, stir once, cover, and simmer for 15–20 minutes or until the water has been absorbed. Remove from the heat and set aside in the covered pan.

2 Heat the oil in a wok or frying pan, add the shallots or onion and chilies and stir-fry for 1–3 minutes. Add the pork, beef, or Canadian bacon and stir-fry for 3 minutes.

3 Add the rice, soy sauce, and tomato paste. Stir-fry for 5–8 minutes, then season with salt to taste.

4 Transfer the rice mixture to a warm serving dish or bowls. Garnish with fried onion rings, strips of omelette, cilantro leaves, and the cucumber slices. Serve immediately.

1½ cups long-grain rice

3 cups water

¼ cup sunflower oil

4 shallots or 1 onion, thinly sliced

2 red chilies, seeded and thinly sliced

2 ounces lean boneless pork, beef, or Canadian bacon, finely diced

2 tablespoons light soy sauce

1 teaspoon tomato paste

salt

To Garnish:

fried onion rings

1 thin omelette, made with 1 egg, cut into strips

cilantro leaves

cucumber slices

Serves 4

Preparation time: 15 minutes

Cooking time: about 25–30 minutes

14

fried rice with ham & bean sprouts

1 Rinse the rice in a sieve under cold running water and drain well. Place the rice in a saucepan, pour in the water, and add salt to taste. Bring to a boil, stir once, cover, and simmer for 15–20 minutes or until the water has been absorbed. Turn the rice out into a sieve and rinse it under cold running water, then set it aside to drain.

2 Heat the oil in a wok or frying pan over a moderate heat and stir-fry the scallions and garlic for about 2 minutes. Add the rice and stir well. Cook gently, stirring continuously as the rice heats through. Stir in the ham and soy sauce.

3 Beat the eggs thoroughly, adding salt and pepper to taste. Pour the eggs into the rice mixture in a thin stream, stirring all the time. Add the bean sprouts and continue cooking, stirring continuously, until the eggs are set and all the ingredients are hot. Serve immediately.

1½ cups long-grain rice

6 cups water

¼ cup sunflower oil

2 scallions, finely chopped

1 garlic clove, crushed

6 ounces cooked ham, diced

¼ cup light soy sauce

2 eggs

2 cups bean sprouts, rinsed and drained

salt and pepper

Serves 4

Preparation time: 15 minutes

Cooking time: 8–10 minutes

■ The rice can be cooked in advance, cooled, and chilled. This is also a quick, tasty dish for using leftover cooked rice.

special egg fried rice

1 Lightly beat the eggs with 1 teaspoon of the scallions and a pinch of salt. Heat ½ tablespoon of the oil in a wok or heavy frying pan and add the eggs. Stir constantly until the eggs are lightly set and scrambled, then transfer them to a bowl and set the mixture aside.

2 Heat the remaining oil in the wok or pan. Add the shrimp, meat, bamboo shoots, peas, and remaining scallions. Stir-fry briskly for about 1 minute, then add the soy sauce and stir-fry for 2–3 minutes.

3 Add the rice to the wok. Replace the scrambled eggs and add salt to taste. Stir well to break up the scrambled eggs and thoroughly reheat and separate the grains of rice. Serve hot, garnished with scallions.

2–3 eggs

2 scallions, finely chopped

⅓ cup vegetable oil

4 ounces cooked, peeled shrimp

4 ounces cooked meat, such as chicken or pork, diced

½ cup canned bamboo shoots, diced

1 cup fresh or frozen peas, cooked

2 tablespoons light soy sauce

1½–2 cups cold, cooked rice

salt

chopped scallions, to garnish

Serves 4	
Preparation time: 15 minutes	
Cooking time: 8–10 minutes	

coconut rice with fish & peas

1 Melt half the butter in a large frying pan. Stir in the coriander, turmeric, cinnamon, and pepper, then add the fish and stir-fry for 1–2 minutes until golden on all sides. Transfer the fish to a bowl using a slotted spoon, taking care not to break up the pieces. Set aside.

2 Melt the remaining butter in the pan and fry the onion and garlic for 5 minutes. Add the rice, stir well until all the grains are glossy, then add the tomatoes, stock, and coconut milk. Bring to the boil, cover, and simmer for 15 minutes.

3 Stir in the peas; taste and adjust the seasoning, if necessary, and arrange the fish on top of the rice. Cover with foil and then the lid and cook for 5 minutes. Leave to stand for a further 5 minutes without removing the foil and lid.

4 Transfer the rice mixture to a warm serving dish. Scatter the cilantro or parsley over the top and add sprigs of cilantro, if using, then serve immediately.

2 tablespoons butter

1 teaspoon ground coriander

½ teaspoon turmeric

½ teaspoon ground cinnamon

½ teaspoon pepper

12 ounces monkfish or skinless cod fillet, cut into bite-sized pieces

1 onion, chopped

1 garlic clove, crushed

1 cup long-grain rice

14-ounce can chopped tomatoes

1½ cups vegetable stock

1 cup coconut milk

1 cup frozen peas, thawed

To Garnish:

2 tablespoons chopped cilantro or parsley

sprigs of cilantro (optional)

Serves 4
Preparation time: 10 minutes
Cooking time: 31–32 minutes

creamy rice with fish

1 Rinse the rice in a sieve under cold running water, then drain well. Bring 3 cups of the chicken stock to a boil in a large saucepan. Add the rice, cover, and cook for 15–20 minutes over a low heat, stirring occasionally. The rice should absorb most of the stock. Add the remaining 4 cups stock, bring back to a boil, then remove the pan from the heat.

2 Heat the oil in a wok, add the garlic and stir-fry until just golden. Use a slotted spoon to remove the garlic and set it aside. Add the cod and stir-fry for 4–6 minutes, adding the ¼ cup stock, if necessary, to keep the fish from sticking.

3 As soon as the cod is cooked, add it to the rice together with the fish sauce and pepper. Mix well and transfer to a serving dish.

4 Garnish the rice mixture with shredded scallions, chopped celery, and the reserved fried garlic. Serve immediately.

¾ cup long-grain rice

7 cups, plus ¼ cup, chicken stock

⅓ cup vegetable oil

2 tablespoons finely chopped garlic

1 pound cod fillet, thinly sliced

3–4 tablespoons fish sauce (nam pla)

1 teaspoon pepper

To Garnish:

2 scallions, shredded

2 celery stalks, very finely chopped

Serves 4

Preparation time: 10 minutes

Cooking time: 30 minutes

pineapple fried rice

1 Rinse the rice in a sieve under cold running water and drain well. Place the rice in a saucepan, pour in the water, and add salt to taste. Bring to a boil, stir once, cover, and simmer for 15–20 minutes or until the water has been absorbed. Turn the rice out into a sieve and rinse it under cold running water, then set it aside and leave to drain.

2 Heat the oil in a wok. Add the garlic and stir-fry until just golden. Add the ham, carrot, raisins, green and red bell pepper, fish sauce, and sugar. Stir-fry for 5 minutes.

3 Add the rice and pineapple. Season the mixture with pepper and stir-fry for a further 5 minutes. Garnish the fried rice with chopped cilantro and serve immediately.

1 cup long-grain rice

3 cups water

½ cup vegetable oil

1 garlic clove, crushed

4 ounces cooked ham, cubed

1 carrot, diced

½ cup raisins

¼ green bell pepper, cored, seeded, and diced

¼ red bell pepper, cored, seeded, and diced

⅓ cup fish sauce (nam pla)

2 tablespoons sugar

4 pineapple rings, diced

salt and pepper

¼ cup chopped cilantro leaves, to garnish

Serves 4
Preparation time: 10 minutes
Cooking time: 25–30 minutes

ten-variety fried rice

1 Rinse the rice in a sieve under cold running water and drain well. Place the rice in a saucepan, pour in the water, and add salt to taste. Bring to a boil, stir once, cover, and simmer for 15–20 minutes or until the water has been absorbed. Turn the rice out into a sieve and rinse it under cold water, then set it aside to drain.

2 Meanwhile, heat 2 tablespoons of the oil in a wok. Add the egg, swirling it around to form a thick skin in the bottom of the wok. When set, turn the omelette out onto a board and leave to cool. Roll up the omelette tightly, slice it finely and set it aside. Mix the sauce ingredients in a bowl.

3 Heat another 2 tablespoons of the oil in the wok, then add the chicken and pork. Stir-fry for 4 minutes over a high heat, until lightly browned. Transfer to a bowl and set aside.

4 Add and heat the remaining oil, then stir-fry the red bell pepper, scallions, garlic, and chilies for 2–3 minutes or until softened.

5 Stir in the tomatoes and cooked rice, then replace the chicken and pork and their juices. Pour in the sauce and toss well over high heat until hot. Fold in the shrimp and crab meat and heat through, shaking the wok occasionally. Top with omelette and garnish with cucumber strips.

¾ cup long-grain rice

3 cups water

⅓ cup vegetable oil

1 egg, beaten

6 ounces boneless, skinless chicken breast, finely sliced

4–6 ounces pork tenderloin, finely sliced

1 red bell pepper, cored, seeded, and finely chopped

4 scallions, finely sliced

2 garlic cloves, crushed

3 green chilies, seeded and finely chopped

3 tomatoes, chopped

4 ounces cooked, peeled shrimp

4 ounces white crab meat, flaked

salt

cucumber strips, to garnish

Sauce:

¾ cup fish stock

¼ cup soy sauce

2 tablespoons superfine sugar

2 teaspoons lemon juice

2 teaspoons fish sauce (nam pla)

Serves 3–4
Preparation time: 25 minutes
Cooking time: 35 minutes

20

chow mein

1 Cook the egg noodles in boiling, salted water for about 5 minutes, or until tender but still firm to the bite (al dente). Cook spaghettini in the same way, allowing slightly longer, according to the packet instructions. Drain the pasta well and rinse under cold running water until cool, then set aside.

2 Heat ⅓ cup of the oil in a wok. Add the onion, meat, snow peas or beans, and the bean sprouts, and stir-fry for about 1 minute. Season the mixture well, stir briefly, then use a slotted spoon to transfer the mixture to a bowl. Keep hot.

3 Heat the remaining oil in the wok and add the scallions and the noodles. Replace about half of the meat and vegetable mixture. Add the soy sauce, then stir-fry for 1–2 minutes, or until completely heated through.

4 Transfer the mixture to a warm serving dish, top with all of the remaining meat and vegetable mixture and sprinkle with the sesame oil or chili sauce (or both if desired). Serve immediately.

1 pound egg noodles or spaghettini

½ cup vegetable oil

1 onion, thinly sliced

4 ounces cooked meat, such as pork, chicken, or ham, finely shredded

4 ounces snow peas or French beans

1 cup bean sprouts

2–3 scallions, finely shredded

¼ cup light soy sauce

2 tablespoons sesame oil or chili sauce

salt

Serves 4

Preparation time: 15 minutes

Cooking time: 15–18 minutes

■ Literally translated, chow mein means "stir-fried noodles." This popular, versatile dish was created by Chinese immigrants in the United States using whatever ingredients they had. Try different combinations of meat and vegetables with the noodles to vary the dish.

1 Cook the noodles in boiling water for 2 minutes. Drain well.

2 Bring the water to a boil in a pan and cook the pork, shrimp, and squid together for 5 minutes. Drain, reserving the cooking liquid.

3 Heat the oil in a wok or frying pan and fry the garlic until golden. Add the bean sprouts and noodles, increase the heat, and stir-fry for 2 minutes.

4 Add the pork mixture, the soy sauces, pepper, and chives, and stir-fry for a further 1 minute. Push the mixture to one side of the pan and add the eggs to the space. Cook them for 1 minute, stirring, then stir in the reserved cooking liquid.

5 Bring to a boil and cook for 2 minutes, stirring well. Transfer to a warmed serving dish and serve.

12 ounces fine egg noodles

2½ cups water

4 ounces lean pork, cut into 2-inch strips

3 ounces uncooked shrimp, shelled

3 ounces prepared squid, sliced

½ cup sunflower oil

2 garlic cloves, crushed

¾ cup bean sprouts

2 tablespoons light soy sauce

2 tablespoons dark soy sauce

½ teaspoon pepper

1 bunch of chives, snipped

2 eggs

Serves 4	
Preparation time: 15 minutes	
Cooking time: 14–18 minutes	

singapore noodles

egg noodles in yellow bean & chili sauce

1 Cook the egg noodles in boiling, salted water for about 5 minutes, or until tender but still firm to the bite (al dente). Cook spaghettini in the same way, according to the packet instructions. Drain the pasta well.

2 Mix the yellow bean paste, chili sauce, and garlic, then set this sauce aside. Heat the oil in a wok or large frying pan over high heat. Add the bell peppers, onion, and bean sprouts and stir-fry for 2 minutes.

3 Add the noodles to the wok and stir in the sauce. Heat through, turning the pasta carefully, then taste and adjust the seasoning if necessary and transfer to a warm serving dish. Serve immediately.

12 ounces egg noodles or spaghettini

⅓ cup yellow bean paste

2 teaspoons chili sauce

1 garlic clove, crushed

⅓ cup vegetable oil

2 green bell peppers, cored, seeded, and cut into thin strips

1 medium onion, thinly sliced

1¼ cups bean sprouts

salt

Serves 4
Preparation time: 10 minutes
Cooking time: 10 minutes

■ Bean sauces are popular in Chinese cooking. Yellow bean sauce is milder than black bean sauce. It is made from salted soy beans, garlic, soy sauce, vinegar, sugar, and seasoning.

thai fried noodles

1 Heat ¼ cup of the oil in a wok. Stir-fry the tofu until brown on all sides. Add the garlic, the noodles, carrot, vinegar, soy sauce, and water, stirring continuously.

2 Push the mixture to one side of the wok and add the eggs to the space. Break the yolks and stir the eggs, gradually incorporating the noodle mixture.

3 Pour the remaining oil down the side of the wok and add the sugar, scallions, and pepper. Cook for 2–3 minutes, stirring and shaking the wok continuously.

4 Heap the noodle mixture onto a plate. Sprinkle the peanuts on top and serve with the bean sprouts and scallion.

⅓ cup peanut oil

6 ounces ready-fried tofu (bean curd), diced

2 tablespoons chopped garlic

4 ounces bean thread noodles, soaked and drained

¼ cup carrot, grated

¼ cup distilled white vinegar or Chinese rice vinegar

¼ cup soy sauce

½ cup water

2 eggs

3 teaspoons sugar

2 scallions, sliced

¼ teaspoon pepper

To Serve:

2 tablespoons crushed roasted peanuts

1 cup bean sprouts

1 scallion, thinly sliced

Serves 2

Preparation time: 15 minutes, plus soaking

Cooking time: 20–25 minutes

noodles with chicken & prawns

1 Soak the dried mushrooms in hot water for 35–40 minutes. Meanwhile, cook the egg noodles in boiling, salted water for 5 minutes, or until tender but still firm to the bite (al dente). Drain the noodles and divide them between 6 bowls. Keep warm.

2 Drain the mushrooms in a sieve. Discard any tough stalks and thinly slice the mushroom caps.

3 Heat the oil in a wok. Add the chicken, garlic, and ginger, and stir-fry over a moderate to high heat for 2–3 minutes. Add the scallions and mushrooms and stir-fry for about 2 minutes.

4 Stir in the shrimp, soy sauce, rice wine or sherry, stock, and salt to taste. Bring to a boil over a high heat, then reduce the heat and simmer for 5 minutes. Blend the cornstarch to a smooth paste with a little cold water, then stir this into the chicken mixture and cook, stirring, until the sauce boils and thickens.

5 Pour the chicken and prawns over the noodles, sprinkle with the shredded ham and serve.

1 ounce dried shiitake mushrooms

1 pound egg noodles

¼ cup peanut oil

6 ounces boneless, skinless chicken breast, diced

1 garlic clove, crushed

2 slices of fresh ginger, peeled and chopped

4 scallions, thinly sliced diagonally into ½-inch pieces

6 ounces uncooked shrimp, peeled

¼ cup soy sauce

¼ cup Chinese rice wine or dry sherry

4 cups chicken stock

¼ cup cornstarch

2 ounces cooked ham, shredded

salt

Serves 6

Preparation time: 20 minutes, plus soaking

Cooking time: 20 minutes

vital vegetables

crispy tofu in tomato sauce

1 Heat the oil in a wok or a deep frying pan. Add the tofu and stir-fry until it is golden brown. Remove from the oil with a slotted spoon and set the tofu aside.

2 Place the tomatoes in a medium saucepan with the stock, fish sauce, salt, and sugar. Bring to a boil, reduce the heat and simmer gently for 15–20 minutes.

3 Add the tofu and simmer for a further 10–15 minutes. The sauce should be thick when ready. Serve immediately, garnished with shredded scallions.

■ For a totally vegetarian dish, use vegetable stock and either totally omit the fish sauce or substitute with a seaweed-based seasoning which is available from health food stores.

oil, for frying

6 pieces of firm tofu (bean curd), halved and cut into bite-size triangles

3 large tomatoes, skinned, seeded, and finely chopped

¾ cup vegetable or chicken stock

2 tablespoons fish sauce (nam pla) (optional)

pinch of salt

⅓ teaspoon sugar

2 shredded scallions, to garnish

Serves 4
Preparation time: 15 minutes
Cooking time: about 40 minutes

three bean stir-fry

1 Heat a wok until hot. Add the oil and heat over a moderate heat until hot. Add the onion and garlic and stir-fry over a gentle heat until the onion has softened slightly.

2 Add the 3 types of beans and increase the heat to high. Toss well to mix then add the strained tomatoes a little at a time, stir-frying after each addition until the tomatoes are evenly combined with the beans.

3 Add the tomato paste, Worcestershire sauce, and sugar; then boil until reduced, stirring the mixture constantly. Remove from the heat, stir in the parsley and salt and pepper to taste. Garnish with parsley sprigs and serve immediately.

¼ cup vegetable oil

1 red onion, finely chopped

2 garlic cloves, crushed

14-ounce can pinto beans, drained and rinsed

14-ounce can red kidney beans, drained and rinsed

14-ounce can cannellini beans, drained and rinsed

2 cups strained tomatoes

¼ cup tomato paste

2 teaspoons Worcestershire sauce

1 teaspoon granulated sugar

½ cup chopped parsley

salt and pepper

parsley sprigs, to garnish

Serves 4
Preparation time: 15 minutes
Cooking time: about 20 minutes

1 Wash the bean sprouts in a bowl of cold water, discarding the husks from the beans and any other particles that float to the surface. Drain well.

2 Heat the oil in a wok until it is smoking hot. Add the scallion, then add the beans and stir a few times. Add the bean sprouts and stir-fry for 30 seconds.

3 Add the sugar and salt to taste, and stir-fry for a further 1 minute. Transfer to a serving dish, sprinkle with the sesame oil and serve immediately.

4 cups bean sprouts

⅓–½ cup sunflower oil

1 scallion, finely chopped

8 ounces dwarf French beans, halved

1 teaspoon sugar

1 teaspoon sesame oil

salt

Serves 4
Preparation time: 10 minutes
Cooking time: 3–4 minutes

bean sprout & green bean stir-fry

■ Fresh bean sprouts are best, preferably bought on the day you plan to use them, as the canned vegetables do not have the same crunchy texture.

eggplant in fragrant sauce

1 Heat the oil for deep-frying in a deep wok or large saucepan to 350–375°F or until a day-old cube of bread browns in 30 seconds. Deep-fry the eggplant for 1–2 minutes, until golden. Use a slotted spoon to remove the eggplant wedges from the pan and place them on paper towels to drain.

2 Carefully pour the oil out of the wok, leaving about 2 tablespoons and reheat this. Quickly stir-fry the scallions, ginger, and garlic. Add the pork, if using, and stir-fry, then stir in the soy sauce, sherry, and chili sauce. Add the eggplant wedges and stir-fry for 1–2 minutes.

3 Mix the cornstarch to a smooth paste with a little water and then stir it into the eggplant mixture. Bring to a boil, stirring, and cook briefly until the sauce thickens. Serve immediately.

vegetable oil, for deep-frying

8 ounces eggplant, peeled and cut into small, thick wedges

2 scallions, chopped

1 slice of fresh ginger, peeled and chopped

1 garlic clove, chopped

4 ounces pork tenderloin, cut into fine strips (optional)

2 tablespoons soy sauce

2 tablespoons dry sherry

2 teaspoons chili sauce

¼ cup cornstarch

Serves 2–3

Preparation time: 15 minutes

Cooking time: about 10 minutes

stir-fried green beans

1 Heat the oil in a wok or large frying pan. Add the garlic, shallots, and ginger. Stir-fry over a moderate heat for 1 minute. Stir in the chili with salt to taste, and continue stir-frying for 30 seconds.

2 Add the green beans and cashew nuts and toss well to combine the ingredients. Stir-fry quickly for 1 minute to brown the cashew nuts.

3 Stir in the stock, sherry, soy sauce, vinegar, and sugar and bring to a boil. Reduce the heat slightly and cook, stirring, for about 4 minutes, until the beans are cooked and the liquid has thickened. Taste and adjust the seasoning if necessary, then serve immediately sprinkled with plenty of black pepper.

⅓ cup oil

2 garlic cloves, crushed

2 shallots, thinly sliced

1 slice of fresh ginger, peeled and chopped

1 red chili, seeded and finely chopped

1 pound green beans, cut into 2-inch lengths

½ cup unsalted cashew nuts

½ cup vegetable or chicken stock

¼ cup dry sherry

2 tablespoons light soy sauce

1 teaspoon vinegar

1 teaspoon sugar

salt and pepper

Serves 4

Preparation time: 10 minutes

Cooking time: 7–8 minutes

■ Shallots have a slightly milder flavor than onion; if they are not available, try using ½ mild white or red salad onion instead of the usual full-flavored and fairly small cooking onions.

stir-fried vegetables

1 Soak the dried mushrooms in warm water for 25–30 minutes. Drain and squeeze the mushrooms, then discard the hard stalks and thinly slice the caps. If using fresh mushrooms, wash and slice them.

2 Heat the oil in a wok or heavy frying pan until it is smoking hot. Reduce the heat and stir-fry the Chinese cabbage and carrots briskly for 30 seconds.

3 Add the beans and mushrooms and continue stir-frying for about 30 seconds. Add the salt and sugar. Toss the vegetables until they are well blended. Stir in the soy sauce and cook for a further 1 minute. Transfer the mixture to a warm serving dish and serve immediately.

5–6 dried shiitake mushrooms or 2 ounces button mushrooms

½ cup vegetable oil

8 ounces Chinese cabbage, thinly sliced diagonally

6 ounces carrots, thinly sliced diagonally

4 ounces French beans, halved if long

1 teaspoon salt

1 teaspoon sugar

2 tablespoons light soy sauce

Serves 3–4

Preparation time: 10 minutes, plus soaking

Cooking time: 3–4 minutes

■ Fresh shiitake mushrooms are usually available from larger supermarkets and they can be used instead of the dried mushrooms. Trim and slice them as with fresh button mushrooms.

stir-fried mixed mushrooms

1 Soak the dried mushrooms in warm water for 25–30 minutes. Drain and squeeze the mushrooms, then discard the hard stalks and thinly slice the caps.

2 Heat the oil in a wok or large frying pan over a moderate heat. Add the ginger, scallions, and the garlic, and stir-fry for 5–10 seconds. Then add the shiitake mushrooms and button mushrooms, and continue stir-frying for 5 minutes.

3 Add the straw mushrooms, chili bean sauce or chili powder, sherry, soy sauce, stock, sugar, salt, and sesame oil. Mix well and then stir-fry for a further 5 minutes. Serve the mushrooms immediately.

2 ounces dried shiitake mushrooms

2 tablespoons oil

1 teaspoon finely chopped fresh ginger

2 scallions, finely chopped

1 garlic clove, crushed

8 ounces button mushrooms, halved or quartered if large

7 ounces canned straw mushrooms, drained

1 teaspoon chili bean sauce or chili powder

2 teaspoons dry sherry

2 teaspoons dark soy sauce

2 tablespoons vegetable or chicken stock

pinch of sugar

pinch of salt

1 teaspoon sesame oil

Serves 4

Preparation time: 5 minutes, plus soaking

Cooking time: 10 minutes

stir-fried vegetable omelette

1 Heat the oil in a wok or frying pan. Stir-fry the onion until softened. Add the garlic, potatoes, bell pepper, and broccoli, and stir-fry for 6 minutes, or until tender but still crisp. (Add a little water if the vegetables start to stick to the pan.)

2 Stir in the tomatoes and chopped cucumber, then spread the mixture out flat. Pour the eggs over the vegetables, stir well, and flatten the mixture again. Cook, without stirring, until the eggs begin to set, then place the pan under a preheated hot broiler until the top of the omelette has set.

3 Cut the omelette into wedges. Sprinkle with parsley and pepper, and serve immediately.

■ Vary the vegetables according to the season—for example, try mushrooms, cooked and drained spinach, bean sprouts, or snow peas. Add a little chopped fresh dill, if liked.

2 tablespoons sunflower oil

1 onion, finely chopped

1 garlic clove, crushed

2 potatoes, quartered and finely sliced

½ green or red bell pepper, cored, seeded, and finely chopped

4–6 broccoli florets

3 tomatoes, sliced

¼ cucumber, chopped

5–6 large eggs, beaten

1 heaped teaspoon chopped parsley

pepper

Serves 4–6
Preparation time: 5 minutes
Cooking time: 10–12 minutes

bok choy in sweet & sour sauce

1 Heat the oil and butter in a wok or a large frying pan. Add the bok choy and sprinkle with the salt. Stir-fry for 2 minutes, then reduce the heat and simmer gently for 5–6 minutes.

2 Meanwhile, in a small saucepan, mix the cornstarch to a smooth paste with the water, then stir in the remaining sauce ingredients. Bring to a boil, reduce the heat and simmer for 4–5 minutes, stirring continuously, until the sauce thickens.

3 Transfer the cabbage to a serving dish and pour the sauce over and serve immediately.

■ Bok choy is widely available at greengrocers and supermarkets. It has a loose head of deep green leaves with short, wide white stalks. The leaves are crisp and juicy in texture, with a mild mustard flavour. Swiss chard can be used instead.

⅓ cup vegetable oil

1 tablespoon butter

2 heads of bok choy, shredded

1 teaspoon salt

Sauce:

3 tablespoons cornstarch

⅔ cup water

3 tablespoons soy sauce

⅓ cup sugar

½ cup vinegar

½ cup orange juice

⅓ cup tomato paste

3 tablespoons Chinese wine or dry sherry

Serves 4
Preparation time: 5 minutes
Cooking time: 11–13 minutes

jumbo shrimp & coconut curry ●

shrimp with thai noodles ●

stir-fried shrimp ●

ginger fish steaks ●

scallop & shrimp stir-fry with mixed vegetables ●

mixed seafood with rice noodles & ginger ●

stir-fried crab with ginger & scallions ●

baby squid stir-fried with fresh herbs ●

stir-fried fish with bacon & vegetables ●

scrambled eggs with shrimp & bean sprouts ●

sweet & sour swordfish ●

fishing for compliments

jumbo shrimp & coconut curry

1 Purée all the ingredients for the spice paste in a blender or spice mill to produce a thick paste. Alternatively, pound the ingredients in a mortar with a pestle.

2 Heat the oil in a wok, add the paste and turmeric, and cook over a gentle heat, stirring frequently, for 3 minutes. Stir in the water and simmer gently for 3 minutes.

3 Stir in the coconut milk, lime juice, sugar, and salt to taste. Simmer for a further 3 minutes. Add the shrimp and stir-fry for 4–5 minutes, or until they turn pink and are cooked.

4 Season the curry to taste, then transfer it to a warmed serving dish. Garnish with scallions and coconut, and serve immediately.

■ Coconut milk is available canned or it can be made by dissolving creamed coconut in hot water. To make coconut milk from fresh or unsweetened coconut flakes, soak grated coconut in boiling water to cover for 30 minutes; drain well and squeeze out the "milk."

¼ cup peanut oil

1 teaspoon turmeric

¾ cup water

¾ cup coconut milk

juice of 1 lime

2 teaspoons light brown sugar

16 uncooked jumbo shrimp, peeled and deveined

salt and pepper

Spice Paste:

2 fresh red chilies, seeded and chopped

2 shallots, chopped

1 lemon grass stalk, chopped

1-inch piece of fresh ginger, peeled and chopped

¼ teaspoon Thai shrimp paste

To Garnish:

4 scallions, cut into thin strips

thin slices of fresh coconut or 2 tablespoons unsweetened coconut flakes

Serves 4
Preparation time: 10 minutes
Cooking time: 15 minutes

8 ounces rice sticks

¼ cup vegetable oil

4 ounces radishes, trimmed and thinly sliced

12 ounces uncooked tiger shrimp, peeled and deveined

juice of 1 lemon

2 tablespoons superfine sugar

2 teaspoons fish sauce (nam pla)

1 teaspoon chili powder, or to taste

salt

To Garnish:

sprigs of Thai sweet basil

2 tablespoons chopped cilantro

Serves 2–3
Preparation time: 10 minutes
Cooking time: 10 minutes

1 Cook or soak the rice sticks in boiling salted water according to the package instructions.

2 Meanwhile, heat the oil in a wok. Add the radishes and stir-fry over high heat for 30 seconds. Add the shrimp and stir-fry for 1–2 minutes or until they just turn pink. Add the lemon juice, sugar, fish sauce, and the chili powder and stir-fry briskly for a further 1–2 minutes.

3 Drain the rice sticks, add them to the shrimp mixture and add salt to taste. Toss until evenly mixed. Serve immediately, garnished with Thai basil and chopped cilantro.

shrimp with thai noodles

stir-fried shrimp

1 Wash the shrimp, remove their heads, shells, and legs, but keep the tails intact. Dry thoroughly on paper towels and set aside.

2 Heat the oil in a wok or large frying pan until it is smoking hot. Add the ginger and fry for 30 seconds to flavor the oil. Use a slotted spoon to remove and discard the ginger.

3 Mix 6 teaspoons of the cornstarch with the salt, sherry, and egg white. Toss the shrimp in this mixture until well coated, then add them to the hot oil and stir-fry until they turn pink. Use a slotted spoon to remove the shrimp from the wok, then set them aside.

4 Add the garlic, black beans, snow peas, and water chestnuts to the oil remaining in the wok and stir-fry for 1–2 minutes, then replace the shrimp. Mix the remaining cornstarch to a smooth paste with the soy sauce and chicken stock, then stir into the shrimp mixture. Cook, stirring, until thickened.

5 Add the sesame oil to the shrimp and toss well. Serve immediately, garnished with scallions and sprigs of cilantro, if using.

1 pound uncooked large shrimp in shells

½ cup vegetable oil

3 slices of fresh ginger, peeled

7 teaspoons cornstarch

1 teaspoon salt

2 tablespoons dry sherry

1 egg white

2 garlic cloves, crushed

2 teaspoons black beans, soaked for 1 hour and drained

8 ounces snow peas, halved

6 water chestnuts, thinly sliced

½ tablespoon soy sauce

¼ cup chicken stock

2 tablespoons sesame oil

To Garnish: (optional)

shredded scallions

sprigs of cilantro

Serves 3–4

Preparation time: 10 minutes, plus soaking

Cooking time: 8–10 minutes

ginger fish steaks

1 Cut the fish steak into bite sized pieces. Mix together the salt, wine or sherry, and 2 tablespoons of the cornstarch, and marinate the fish in this mixture for about 30 minutes.

2 Dip the marinated fish pieces in the egg white, then in the remaining cornstarch. Heat the oil in a wok or frying pan until hot, then fry the fish until golden, stirring occasionally.

3 Add the ginger, soy sauce, sugar, and stock or water. Cook for about 3–4 minutes, or until the liquid has evaporated. Serve hot, garnished with the shredded scallion.

■ Coating the fish in egg white and cornstarch before adding it to the wok or pan helps prevent the fish from breaking up during stir-frying.

1 pound fish steak, such as cod, halibut, or hake

½ teaspoon salt

¼ cup Chinese wine or dry sherry

½ cup cornstarch

1 egg white, lightly beaten

⅓ cup sunflower oil

1 slice of fresh ginger, peeled and finely chopped

¼ cup light soy sauce

2 teaspoons sugar

½ cup chicken stock or water

shredded scallion, to garnish

Serves 4
Preparation time: 15 minutes, plus marinating
Cooking time: 15–20 minutes

scallop & shrimp stir-fry with mixed vegetables

1 Cut each scallop into 3–4 pieces and place in a bowl. Leave the shrimp whole if small, otherwise cut each into 2–3 pieces; add to the scallops. Add the egg white and about half the cornstarch, then mix well.

2 Heat the oil for deep-frying in a wok or saucepan to 350–375°F or until a day-old cube of bread browns in 30 seconds. Deep-fry the scallops and shrimp for 1 minute, stirring them all the time with chop-sticks to keep the pieces separate. Use a slotted spoon to remove the scallops and shrimp out of the oil and drain them on paper towels.

3 Pour off all but ¼ cup oil from the wok. Increase the heat to high and add the ginger and scallions. Add the celery, bell pepper, and carrots, and stir-fry for about 1 minute, then replace the scallops and shrimp. Stir in the wine or sherry, soy sauce, chili bean paste, if using, and season to taste with salt.

4 Mix the remaining cornstarch to a smooth paste with a little water, then pour this into the wok and cook, stirring, until the sauce boils and thickens. Sprinkle the sesame seed oil over the mixture and serve immediately.

4–6 fresh scallops

4–6 ounces uncooked shrimp, peeled and deveined

1 egg white

2 tablespoons cornstarch

vegetable oil, for deep-frying

2 slices of fresh ginger, peeled and finely shredded

2–3 scallions, finely shredded

3 celery stalks, sliced

1 red bell pepper, cored, seeded, and diced

1–2 carrots, sliced

¼ cup Chinese wine or dry sherry

2 tablespoons light soy sauce

2 teaspoons chili bean paste (optional)

1 teaspoon sesame oil

salt

Serves 4–6

Preparation time: 20–25 minutes

Cooking time: 6–8 minutes

mixed seafood with rice noodles & ginger

1 Soak the mushrooms in warm water for 15–20 minutes. Drain and squeeze the mushrooms, then discard the hard stalks and thinly slice the caps.

2 Cook or soak the rice noodles according to package instructions, until they are just tender. Drain and rinse in cold water, then set aside.

3 Heat the oil in a wok or a large frying pan. Add the scallions, garlic, and ginger and stir-fry briskly for 30 seconds. Stir in the mushrooms, shrimp, and squid, if using, then cook for 2 minutes.

4 Add the clams, wine or sherry, soy sauce, and season to taste with salt. Carefully stir in the noodles and heat through, then transfer the mixture into a warm dish and serve immediately.

4 dried shiitake mushrooms

1 pound rice noodles

¼ cup vegetable oil

4 scallions, chopped

2 garlic cloves, sliced

1 piece of fresh ginger, peeled and finely chopped

2 ounces cooked, peeled shrimp, thawed if frozen

4 ounces squid rings (optional)

8-ounce can clams, drained

¼ cup Chinese wine or dry sherry

2 tablespoons soy sauce

salt

Serves 4–6

Preparation time: 10 minutes, plus soaking

Cooking time: about 10 minutes

¼ cup cornstarch

¼ cup Chinese wine or dry sherry

2 tablespoons chicken stock or water

⅓ cup sunflower oil

meat from 1 crab, about 1¾ pounds in weight

4 slices of fresh ginger, peeled and finely chopped

4 scallions, finely chopped

1 teaspoon salt

1 teaspoon light soy sauce

2 teaspoons sugar

1 Mix the cornstarch to a smooth paste with half the wine or sherry and the stock or water. Add the crab and stir, taking care not to break it up too much. Leave to marinate for about 10 minutes.

2 Heat the oil in a wok or frying pan. Add the crab and stir-fry for 1 minute. Add the ginger, scallions, salt, soy sauce, sugar, and the remaining wine or sherry. Cook for about 5 minutes, stirring constantly. Add a little water if the mixture becomes very dry. Serve immediately.

Serves 4

Preparation time: 25–30 minutes, plus marinating

Cooking time: 6 minutes

stir-fried crab with ginger & scallions

■ Fresh crabs are a favorite ingredient in Chinese cooking. Most fishmongers sell prepared crab meat on the shell— buy 2 if they are small.

baby squid stir-fried with fresh herbs

1 To prepare the squid, hold the head and tentacles in one hand and pull away the body with the other. Pull the innards and the hard "pen" away from the body and discard. Cut the tentacles from the head: reserve the tentacles and discard the head.

2 Sprinkle some salt on your fingers and rub the thin mottled skin from the body and tentacles. Rinse well and pat dry. Cut the flesh into slices. Season with salt and pepper.

3 Heat the oil in a wok over a gentle heat. Add the garlic and cook until browned. Remove with a slotted spoon and discard.

4 Increase the heat. When the oil is hot, add the squid and cook briskly for 1 minute, stirring to keep the pieces from sticking together. Add the cilantro, parsley, and lemon juice, and stir-fry for 30 seconds.

5 Transfer to a warm serving dish. Garnish, if desired, with slices or grated zest of lemon or lime and tiny sprigs of cilantro or parsley and serve immediately.

2 pounds baby squid

½ cup sunflower oil

3–4 garlic cloves, sliced

¼ cup chopped cilantro

2 tablespoons chopped Italian parsley

juice of ½ lemon

salt and pepper

To Garnish: (optional)

slices or grated zest of lemon or lime

tiny sprigs of cilantro or parsley

Serves 4
Preparation time: about 10 minutes
Cooking time: 2–4 minutes

■ Baby squid is the best to use for stir-frying, as its flesh is delicate and very tender. It must be cooked quickly or it becomes tough. It is ideal for stir-fried dishes such as this.

stir-fried fish with bacon & vegetables

1 Place the fish in a dish, sprinkle with the salt and leave to stand for 15 minutes. Drain, if necessary, and pat dry on paper towels.

2 Heat the oil in a wok or large frying pan over a moderate heat. Add the fish and bacon and stir-fry for 3 minutes.

3 Add the peas, corn, stock or water, wine or sherry, soy sauce, and sugar. Bring to a boil. Blend the cornstarch to a thin paste with a little water and add to the sauce, stirring continuously, then cook for 1 minute.

4 Transfer to a warm dish and garnish with lemon slices, if using, and scallion, and serve.

1 pound skinless cod fillet, cut into wide strips

1 teaspoon salt

2 tablespoons oil

2–3 slices of Canadian bacon, cut into fine strips

½ cup peas, cooked

½ cup corn kernels, cooked

¾ cup chicken stock or water

¼ cup Chinese wine or dry sherry

2 teaspoons light soy sauce

1 teaspoon sugar

1 teaspoon cornstarch

To Garnish:

lemon slices (optional)

finely shredded scallion

Serves 4
Preparation time: 5 minutes, plus standing
Cooking time: 5–7 minutes

scrambled eggs with shrimp & bean sprouts

1 Beat the eggs with the soy sauce. Heat the oil in a wok or a large frying pan over a high heat.

2 Add the onions, garlic, and bean sprouts and stir-fry for 1 minute. Mix in the eggs and shrimp. Cook, stirring constantly, until the eggs start to scramble. Serve hot, garnished with scallion, if using.

8 eggs

⅓ cup soy sauce

½ cup oil

2 medium onions, thinly sliced

1 garlic clove, finely chopped

1¼ cups bean sprouts

4 ounces shelled shrimp

chopped scallion, to garnish

Serves 4
Preparation time: 10 minutes
Cooking time: 5–6 minutes

■ Bean sprouts are the sprouts of small green mung beans. Although they are available in cans, it is best to use them fresh if possible. You can grow your own beansprouts by putting some mung beans in a jam jar, covering it with cheesecloth and securing it with a rubber band. Rinse the beans every day until the sprouts are large enough.

sweet & sour swordfish

1 Mix all the ingredients for the marinade in a shallow dish. Add the swordfish and turn the pieces to coat them evenly. Cover and leave to marinate for about 30 minutes, turning the fish occasionally.

2 Heat the wok until hot. Add ¼ cup of the oil and heat until hot. Use a slotted spoon to remove the swordfish strips from the marinade, draining off as much liquid as possible, and add them to the pan. Reserve the marinade. Stir-fry the swordfish for 3–5 minutes, or until tender. Remove the wok from the heat and use a slotted spoon to transfer the swordfish to a plate. Set aside.

3 Mix the cornstarch to a paste with a little of the fish stock, then stir in the reserved marinade and the remaining stock. Set aside.

4 Return the wok to a moderate heat. Add the remaining oil and heat until hot. Stir-fry the bell pepper strips for 5 minutes. Stir the cornstarch mixture, then pour it into the wok and bring to a boil, stirring continuously.

5 Return the swordfish and its juices to the wok. Increase the heat and stir-fry for 1–2 minutes or until all the ingredients are combined and hot. Serve with rice or noodles.

1 pound swordfish fillet, cut into chunky strips

⅓ cup vegetable oil

2 tablespoons cornstarch

½ cup cold fish stock

1 green bell pepper, cored, seeded, and cut into thin strips

1 red pepper, cored, seeded, and cut into thin strips

Marinade:

⅓ cup soy sauce

¼ cup Chinese wine or dry sherry

2 tablespoons red or white wine vinegar

1 tablespoon light brown sugar

Serves 4
Preparation time: 15 minutes, plus marinating
Cooking time: 9–12 minutes

tangy fried chicken livers with broccoli ●

chicken with green peppers ●

ginger chicken with honey ●

chicken chop suey ●

fried eight-piece chicken ●

stir-fried sesame chicken ●

chicken with shrimp sauce ●

chicken with pineapple ●

lemon chicken ●

malaysian orange chicken ●

ginger chicken with baby mushrooms ●

bang bang chicken ●

stir-fried duck with bamboo shoots & almonds ●

oriental duckling ●

sesame marinated turkey ●

more than
chicken

58

tangy fried chicken livers with broccoli

1 Heat the oil and butter in a wok or large frying pan. Stir-fry the garlic for 1 minute. Add the mushrooms and chicken livers and cook for 5 minutes, stirring occasionally, until the chicken livers are browned.

2 Add the broccoli, orange zest and juice, sherry, and ground ginger. Season the mixture with a little salt and plenty of pepper. Bring to a boil, reduce the heat, cover, and simmer for 5–6 minutes, or until the broccoli is just tender but still crisp.

3 Adjust the seasoning to taste and transfer to a serving dish. Garnish with parsley and serve immediately, with boiled rice, if liked.

¼ cup sesame oil

2 tablespoons butter

2 garlic cloves, crushed

8 ounces mushrooms, thinly sliced

1 pound chicken livers, roughly chopped

4 ounces broccoli, roughly chopped

2 tablespoons grated orange zest

½ cup orange juice

¼ cup dry sherry

pinch of ground ginger

salt and pepper

¼ cup chopped parsley, to garnish

Serves 4

Preparation time: 20 minutes

Cooking time: 11–12 minutes

chicken with green peppers

1 Season the chicken with ½ teaspoon of the salt, then mix it with the egg white and add 2 teaspoons of the cornstarch. Mix well. Blend the remaining cornstarch to a smooth paste with a little water.

2 Heat the oil in a wok or a large frying pan. Stir-fry the chicken over a moderate heat until it turns white, then remove from the wok with a slotted spoon and set aside.

3 Increase the heat to high. When the oil is very hot, add the scallion and ginger. Add the peppers and stir-fry for 30 seconds, then replace the chicken and add the remaining salt and the rice wine or sherry. Stir-fry for 1 minute.

4 Pour in the cornstarch paste, stirring, and cook briefly until the liquid has thickened. Serve garnished with sesame seeds, scallion strips, lime wedges, and chili slices.

2 boneless, skinless chicken breasts, cut into thin strips

1½ teaspoons salt

1 egg white, lightly beaten

3 teaspoons cornstarch

½ cup vegetable oil

1 scallion, finely chopped

2 slices of fresh ginger, peeled and finely chopped

8 ounces green bell peppers, cored, seeded, and cut into short thin strips

¼ cup rice wine or dry sherry

To Garnish:

1 teaspoon sesame seeds

scallion strips

lime wedges

red chili slices

Serves 4
Preparation time: 10–15 minutes
Cooking time: 10 minutes

2 ounces fresh ginger, peeled and finely chopped

¼ cup vegetable oil

3 boneless, skinless chicken breasts, chopped

3 chicken livers, chopped

1 onion, finely sliced

3 garlic cloves, crushed

2 ounces dried black fungus (cloud's ears), soaked in hot water for 20 minutes and drained

2 tablespoons soy sauce

2 tablespoons honey

5 scallions, chopped

1 red chili, seeded and cut into fine strips, to garnish

rice sticks, to serve (optional)

1 Place the ginger in a small bowl. Add a little cold water, mix well, then drain and squeeze the ginger until it is dry.

2 Heat the oil in a wok. Stir-fry the chopped chicken and livers over a moderate heat for 5 minutes. Use a slotted spoon to remove the chicken mixture from the wok and set aside.

3 Add the onion and fry gently until soft, then add the garlic and the drained black fungus, and stir-fry for 1 minute. Return the chicken mixture to the wok.

4 Stir the soy sauce and honey in a bowl until blended, then pour this over the chicken and stir well. Add the ginger and stir-fry for 2–3 minutes. Add the scallions and serve, garnished with strips of chili and accompanied by rice sticks, if liked.

Serves 4

Preparation time: 15 minutes, plus soaking

Cooking time: 10–15 minutes

ginger chicken with honey

■ This dish tastes even better if cooked the day before, cooled and chilled, then thoroughly reheated before being served.

chicken chop suey

1 Heat 2 tablespoons of the oil, add the scallions and ginger, and stir-fry for 1 minute.

2 Add the garlic and chicken, and stir-fry for 2 minutes. Lower the heat, and add the tomato paste, the wine or sherry, soy sauce, sugar, and ⅔ cup of the water.

3 Heat through gently, then transfer to a warm serving dish. Heat 2 teaspoons of the oil in the pan, add the bean sprouts and remaining water, and stir-fry for 3 minutes.

4 Add to the serving dish and keep warm. Wipe out the pan and heat the remaining oil. Pour in the beaten eggs and cook gently until set and crisp. Cut into thin strips and place on top of the bean sprout mixture and serve immediately.

¼ cup oil

5 scallions, chopped

1-inch piece fresh ginger, peeled and chopped

2 garlic cloves, crushed

6 ounces chicken breast, skinned and cut into thin strips

2 tablespoons tomato paste

¼ cup Chinese wine or dry sherry

¼ cup soy sauce

1 teaspoon sugar

1 cup water

2½ cups bean sprouts

3 eggs, beaten with ¼ cup water

Serves 4
Preparation time: 8 minutes
Cooking time: 8–10 minutes

■ The term Chop Suey comes from the Chinese word "zasui" which means "mixed bits." Small portions of meat, fish, and vegetables can be added—a great way to use up leftovers.

fried
eight-piece
chicken

1 Carefully cut off the legs, wings, and breasts from the chicken. Then cut each breast in half.

2 In a bowl large enough to hold all the chicken, mix the scallions and ginger with 2 tablespoons of the sherry, 1 teaspoon of the sugar, and 2 tablespoons of the soy sauce. Turn the chicken in this marinade until it is well coated. Cover and leave to marinate for about 5 minutes.

3 Remove the chicken from the marinade, draining each piece well, and dust with cornstarch. Reserve any leftover marinade.

4 Heat the butter or lard in a wok or large frying pan. Fry the chicken over moderate heat until golden brown and cooked through. Pour off the excess lard, leaving the chicken in the wok.

5 Add the remaining sherry, sugar, soy sauce, and leftover marinade. Bring to a boil, stirring. Stir in the sesame oil and serve immediately, garnished with chives.

2½-pound spring chicken, rinsed and dried

2–3 scallions, finely chopped

2–3 slices of fresh ginger, peeled and finely chopped

¼ cup dry sherry

2 tablespoons sugar

⅓ cup soy sauce

⅓ cup cornstarch

½ cup butter or lard

1 teaspoon sesame oil

snipped chives, to garnish

Serves 4
Preparation time: 20 minutes
Cooking time: 15 minutes

1 Place the chicken in a bowl, sprinkle with the cornstarch and toss until all the pieces are evenly coated. Heat the oil in a wok and stir-fry the chicken over a high heat for 45 seconds. Use a slotted spoon to remove the chicken from the wok and set aside.

2 Add the bell pepper and stir-fry over moderate heat for 1 minute. Stir in 2 tablespoons of the soy sauce, then remove the bell pepper with a slotted spoon and set aside.

3 Add the remaining soy sauce, the sesame seed paste, sesame oil, stock or water, chili sauce, and sherry. Cook, stirring, for 1 minute, then replace the chicken and stir over a high heat for about 45 seconds. Stir in the reserved bell pepper and cook for a further 30 seconds or until the pepper is just tender.

4 Transfer the chicken mixture to a serving dish and garnish with the sesame seeds. Serve immediately.

1 pound boneless, skinless chicken breasts, cut into 1-inch cubes

1½ teaspoons cornstarch

½ cup vegetable oil

1 green bell pepper, cored, seeded, and cut into 1-inch pieces

⅓ cup soy sauce

⅓ cup sesame seed paste

2 tablespoons sesame oil

2 tablespoons chicken stock or water

1 teaspoon chili sauce

2 tablespoons dry sherry

sesame seeds, to garnish

Serves 3–4

Preparation time: 10 minutes

Cooking time: 7–8 minutes

stir-fried sesame chicken

chicken with shrimp sauce

1 Cut the chicken pieces into small portions, each about 1½ inches long. Purée the onion, garlic, ginger, and chilies with the water in a food processor or blender.

2 Heat the oil in a wok and fry the onion purée for 3–4 minutes. Add the turmeric, pepper, shrimp paste, and laos powder, if using, and cook briskly for 1 minute. Add the lemon zest, fish sauce, salt, and chicken pieces and stir-fry until the chicken starts to brown.

3 Pour in the coconut milk, then stir in the sugar and bring to a boil. Simmer, covered, for 30 minutes or until the chicken is cooked through and tender. Stir in the lemon juice and serve immediately.

3 pounds chicken pieces

1 onion, quartered

4 garlic cloves, peeled

1-inch piece of fresh ginger, peeled and chopped

3 fresh red chilies, seeded and quartered

2 tablespoons water

⅓ cup sunflower oil

1 teaspoon turmeric

1 teaspoon pepper

½ teaspoon dried shrimp paste

½ teaspoon laos powder (optional)

2 strips of lemon zest

2 teaspoons fish sauce (nam pla)

1½ teaspoons salt

1½ cups coconut milk

2 tablespoons sugar

¼ cup lemon juice

Serves 4

Preparation time: 20 minutes

Cooking time: about 40 minutes

■ Chicken thighs are ideal for this recipe; use a meat cleaver to chop each into 2 or 3 smaller portions.

chicken with pineapple

1 Cut the chicken into bite-sized pieces. Using a fork, whisk the egg white with a little salt and pepper until frothy. Sift in the cornstarch and whisk until well mixed, then add the chicken and stir until coated.

2 Heat the oil in a wok until very hot but not smoking. Stir-fry about a quarter of the chicken for 30–60 seconds, until the chicken turns white. Use a slotted spoon to remove the chicken and drain on paper towels. Repeat with the remaining chicken. Carefully pour off all but about 2 tablespoons of the hot oil from the wok.

3 Return the wok to a low heat and make the sauce: stir-fry the onion, carrot, and ginger for 3 minutes or until softened but not browned. Pour in the stock or water, orange and lemon juices, and increase the heat. Bring to a boil, stirring, then stir in the soy sauce, vinegar, and 1 teaspoon of sugar.

4 Put the chicken in the sauce and cook over a moderate to high heat, stirring occasionally, for about 3 minutes. Add the pineapple and juice and cook for 1 minute.

5 Blend the cornstarch to a smooth paste with a little cold water. Add to the chicken and simmer, stirring, for 2 minutes, until thickened. Season to taste, adding more sugar if desired. Serve hot, garnished with carrot or orange zest and scallion strips.

2 boneless, skinless chicken breasts, about 8–10 ounces total weight

1 egg white

2 teaspoons cornstarch

⅓ cup peanut oil

4 ounces prepared pineapple, cut into bite-sized pieces, with juice reserved

salt and pepper

Sauce:

1 small onion, cut into chunks

1 carrot, cut into short fine strips

1-inch piece of fresh ginger, peeled and cut into fine strips

¾ cup cold chicken stock or water

1 cup orange juice

¼ cup lemon juice

2 tablespoons light soy sauce

2 tablespoons white wine vinegar

1–2 teaspoons sugar, to taste

2 teaspoons cornstarch

To Garnish:

fine strips of carrot or orange zest

fine strips of scallion

Serves 2–4
Preparation time: 15 minutes
Cooking time: about 20 minutes

lemon chicken

1 First prepare the sauce. Mix the cornstarch to a thin paste with the stock or water, then add the remaining sauce ingredients, stirring well.

2 In a shallow dish, lightly beat the egg white with the cornstarch and salt. Add the strips of chicken and turn them to coat with the egg white mixture. Set aside.

3 Heat the oil in a wok until hot but not smoking. Use a fork to add the strips of chicken individually into the hot oil. Stir-fry for 3–4 minutes or until golden—do this in batches as the pieces will not cook evenly if too many are added at once. Use a slotted spoon to remove the chicken and drain the pieces on paper towels. Keep hot.

4 Pour off all but 2 tablespoons oil from the wok. Stir-fry the scallions and garlic over a moderate heat for 30 seconds. Stir the sauce and pour it into the wok, stirring continuously. Increase the heat to high and bring to a boil, stirring.

5 Return the chicken to the wok and stir-fry for 1–2 minutes or until evenly coated in the sauce. Garnish with lemon slices and serve.

1 egg white

2 teaspoons cornstarch

pinch of salt

2 boneless, skinless chicken breasts, about 10 ounces total weight, cut across the grain into thin strips

1½ cups vegetable oil

½ bunch of scallions, shredded

1 garlic clove, crushed

lemon slices, to garnish

Sauce:

2 teaspoons cornstarch

½ cup cold chicken stock or water

finely grated zest of ½ lemon

¼ cup lemon juice

2 tablespoons soy sauce

2 teaspoons rice wine or dry sherry

2 teaspoons superfine sugar

Serves 2
Preparation time: 15 minutes
Cooking time: 4–6 minutes

1 Using a fork, lightly whisk the egg whites with the cornstarch and a pinch of salt in a shallow dish. Add the chicken and turn the strips to coat them evenly. Mix all the ingredients for the sauce and set aside.

2 Heat the oil in a wok until hot but not smoking. Use a fork to add the strips of chicken individually to the hot oil. Fry for 3–4 minutes or until golden—you will have to do this in batches as the pieces will not cook evenly if too many are added at once. Use a slotted spoon to remove the chicken and drain the pieces on paper towels. Keep hot.

3 Pour off almost all the oil from the wok. Add the scallions and stir-fry briskly over a moderate heat for 30 seconds. Pour in the sauce and bring to a boil, stirring, then add the peas and salt and pepper to taste. Simmer, stirring frequently, for about 5 minutes or until the peas are cooked.

4 Replace the chicken in the wok and toss for 1–2 minutes or until all the ingredients are well combined and piping hot. Serve garnished with orange slices and flat leaf parsley.

2 egg whites

2 tablespoons cornstarch

4 boneless, skinless chicken breasts, about 1¼ pounds total weight, cut across the grain into thin strips

1½ cups vegetable oil

1 bunch of scallions, thinly sliced diagonally

1 cup fresh or frozen peas

salt and pepper

Sauce:

¾ cup fresh orange juice

⅓–½ cup concentrated frozen orange juice, or to taste

¼ cup soy sauce

2 tablespoons cider vinegar

1 teaspoon soft brown sugar

To Garnish:

orange slices

sprigs of flat leaf parsley

Serves 3–4
Preparation time: 15 minutes
Cooking time: 10–15 minutes

malaysian orange chicken

ginger chicken
with baby mushrooms

1 Place the chicken pieces in a bowl, sprinkle with the sugar and leave to stand for 20–30 minutes. Season with salt and pepper. Blend the cornstarch to a smooth paste with ⅓ cup of water and set aside.

2 Heat the oil in a wok and fry the ginger for 1 minute. Add the chicken and stir-fry for 3 minutes.

3 Pour in the remaining water and stir in the mushrooms. Bring to a boil, then reduce the heat. Cover and simmer for 5 minutes or until the chicken is tender.

4 Add the brandy, soy sauce, and season to taste. Stir the corn-starch mixture and pour it into the chicken, stirring. Bring to a boil, stirring, and cook for about 30–60 seconds or until the sauce is thickened; then serve hot.

1½ pounds boneless, skinless chicken breasts, cut into finger-sized pieces

1 teaspoon sugar

2 teaspoons cornstarch

½ cup sesame oil

4-inch piece of fresh ginger, peeled and finely sliced

⅓ –½ cup, plus 3 tablespoons, water

4 ounces button mushrooms

¼ cup brandy

1 teaspoon light soy sauce

salt and pepper

Serves 4

Preparation time: 10 minutes, plus standing

Cooking time: 10–15 minutes

bang bang chicken

1 Place the chicken breasts between 2 sheets of greaseproof paper and bang hard with a rolling pin to flatten and tenderize them. Cut the chicken into thin strips across the grain, then place in a shallow dish. Mix ¼ cup of the soy sauce with the sesame oil and ginger. Pour over the chicken and turn to coat. Cover and leave to marinate for 15 minutes.

2 Meanwhile, heat the wok until hot. Dry-fry the sesame seeds over a gentle heat for 1–2 minutes or until toasted, tossing so they do not burn. Remove the wok from the heat and empty the seeds onto a plate.

3 Return the wok to a moderate heat with half of the vegetable oil. Add the carrots and chili and stir-fry for 2–3 minutes. Remove with a slotted spoon and place in a bowl. Add the bean sprouts to the wok and stir-fry for 1 minute, then transfer the bean sprouts into a bowl. Add the cucumber strips and toss well.

4 Heat the remaining oil in the wok. Add the chicken, increase the heat and stir-fry for 4–5 minutes. Transfer the chicken to a separate bowl. Add the remaining soy sauce, the rice wine or sherry, honey, and stock to the wok. Bring to a boil, stirring, then simmer briefly, stirring constantly, until reduced slightly. Pour half of the sauce over the vegetables and half over the chicken. Stir to mix, then cover and leave to cool, stirring occasionally.

5 Arrange the mixtures on plates, drizzle any remaining sauce over them and sprinkle with the sesame seeds. Garnish with parsley and serve.

4 large boneless, skinless chicken breasts

¾ cup soy sauce

¼ cup sesame oil

1-inch piece of fresh ginger, peeled and finely chopped

¼ cup sesame seeds

½ cup vegetable oil

4 carrots, cut into julienne strips

1 fresh green or red chili, seeded and chopped

1 cup bean sprouts

½ cucumber, cut into julienne strips

⅓ cup rice wine or dry sherry

¼ cup clear honey

¾ cup chicken stock

flat leaf parsley, to garnish

Serves 4

Preparation time: about 30 minutes, plus cooling

Cooking time: about 15 minutes

stir-fried duck with bamboo shoots & almonds

1 Place the duck in a large bowl with the ginger and garlic. Add 2 tablespoons of the oil, mix well, and leave to marinate for 30 minutes.

2 Soak the mushrooms in warm water for 15 minutes, then drain and squeeze them dry. Discard the stalks and slice the mushroom caps.

3 Heat the remaining oil in a wok or large frying pan and stir-fry the scallions for 30 seconds. Add the duck and stir-fry for 2 minutes. Add the mushrooms, bamboo shoots, soy sauce, and wine or sherry, and cook for 2 minutes.

4 Blend the cornstarch to a smooth paste with the water and stir into the duck mixture. Cook for 1 minute, stirring, until thickened. Stir in the almonds and serve immediately.

1 pound boneless, skinless duck breast, cut into small chunks

2 slices of fresh ginger, peeled and shredded

1 garlic clove, crushed

⅓ cup sesame oil

3–4 dried shiitake mushrooms

4 scallions, sliced

4 ounces canned bamboo shoots, drained and sliced

⅓ cup soy sauce

¼ cup Chinese wine or dry sherry

2 teaspoons cornstarch

2 tablespoons water

¼ cup flaked almonds, toasted

Serves 4–6

Preparation time: 15 minutes, plus marinating and soaking

Cooking time: 6–7 minutes

oriental duckling

1 Check the weight of the duckling and calculate the cooking time at 30 minutes per pound. Prick the duckling all over with a fork and place in a roasting tin. Sprinkle with salt and roast in a preheated oven, 375°F, for the calculated cooking time, until golden brown and cooked through. Leave to cool, then strip the flesh and skin from the carcass and cut into thin strips.

2 Heat ¼ cup of the oil in a wok or large frying pan. Add the onion, mushrooms, garlic, and peppers and stir-fry for 4 minutes. Use a slotted spoon to transfer the mixture to a plate and keep warm.

3 Heat the remaining oil in the wok or pan. Stir-fry the meat and skin with the bean sprouts for 3 minutes. Remove from the wok; keep warm.

4 Blend the cornstarch to a smooth paste with the soy sauce and sherry, then stir in the stock. Pour this sauce into the wok and bring to a boil, stirring. Reduce the heat and simmer for 2 minutes.

5 Stir in the almonds and add the cooked ingredients. Taste and adjust the seasoning. Heat through for 3 minutes, then serve with boiled rice or crisp-fried noodles, if desired.

4-pound oven-ready duckling

⅔ cup corn oil

1 large onion, thinly sliced

4 ounces button mushrooms, thickly sliced

1 garlic clove, crushed

1 small red bell pepper, cored, seeded, and cut into thin strips

1 small green bell pepper, cored, seeded, and cut into thin strips

2 cups bean sprouts

2 tablespoons cornstarch

2 tablespoons soy sauce

2–3 teaspoons dry sherry

1½ cups chicken stock

1 cup blanched almonds, toasted

salt and pepper

Serves 4
Preparation time: 30 minutes
Cooking time: 2 hours 12 minutes

sesame marinated turkey

1 Mix all the marinade ingredients in a bowl. Add the turkey cubes and turn them in the marinade until they are thoroughly coated. Cover and leave in a cool place for 30 minutes.

2 Meanwhile, heat the oil in a wok or large frying pan. Stir-fry the cashew nuts until golden brown. Use a slotted spoon to remove the nuts from the pan and drain on paper towels, then set aside and keep warm.

3 Add the turkey and its marinade and stir-fry for 2 minutes. Add the mushrooms and cook for 1 minute. Transfer the mixture to warm plates, sprinkle with the cashews, scallions, and red bell pepper and serve.

1 pound boneless, skinless turkey breast, cut into small cubes

2 tablespoons vegetable oil

1 cup unsalted cashew nuts

3 ounces button or shiitake mushrooms, halved

Sesame Marinade:

3 scallions, chopped

⅓ cup soy sauce

¼ cup chili oil

¼ cup sesame oil

2 tablespoons sesame seed paste

1 teaspoon ground Szechuan pepper

To Serve:

1–2 scallions, finely shredded

1 red bell pepper, cored, seeded, and finely shredded

Serves 4
Preparation time: 10 minutes, plus marinating
Cooking time: 6–7 minutes

lamb with spicy hot sauce ●
lamb & zucchini fritters ●
spring lamb stir-fried with garlic ●
fried pork with baby corn & snow peas ●
sweet & sour pork ●
spicy pork meatballs ●
stir-fried pork with eggplant ●
pork with bean sprouts ●
szechuan dry-fried shredded beef ●
beef with broccoli ●
stir-fried beef with plum sauce & mushrooms ●
fried beef with french beans ●
stir-fried liver & spinach ●
stir-fried beef in hot chili sauce ●

for meat's sake

lamb with spicy hot sauce

1 First prepare the ingredients for the sauce. Blend the cornstarch to a thin paste with the cold water, then stir in the chili sauce, vinegar, sugar, and five-spice powder.

2 Heat ¼ cup of the oil in a wok. Stir-fry the lamb over a high heat for 3–4 minutes or until browned on all sides. Transfer the lamb and its juices to a bowl.

3 Reduce the heat to moderate. Add the remaining oil and heat until hot, then stir-fry the scallions and garlic for 30 seconds. Remove with a slotted spoon.

4 Stir the sauce to combine the ingredients, then pour it into the wok and increase the heat to high. Bring to a boil, stirring, and cook briefly until the sauce thickens.

5 Add the lamb and its juices, and the scallion mixture. Toss the ingredients in the sauce until piping hot. Garnish with a few small chilies, if using, and serve immediately, with noodles.

⅓ cup peanut oil

1 pound lamb neck fillet, trimmed and cut across the grain into thin strips

4 scallions, sliced diagonally

2 garlic cloves, crushed

6–8 small red chilies, to garnish (optional)

bean thread noodles, to serve

Sauce:

2 teaspoons cornstarch

½ cup cold water

¼ cup hot chili sauce

2 tablespoons rice wine vinegar, white wine vinegar, or cider vinegar

2 teaspoons dark brown sugar

½ teaspoon five-spice powder

Serves 3–4
Preparation time: 10 minutes
Cooking time: about 10 minutes

lamb & zucchini fritters

1 Coat the zucchini rounds in the seasoned flour. Put the sesame seeds in a wok or a large frying pan and dry-fry over a moderate heat for 1–2 minutes until toasted; remove from the pan and set aside.

2 Mix the ground lamb with the scallion, garlic, and toasted sesame seeds. Press this mixture onto one side of each zucchini round, then coat the rounds in more flour.

3 Heat the oil in the wok to 350–375°F or until a cube of day-old bread browns in 30 seconds. Gently dip the zucchini rounds into the beaten eggs a few at a time, then fry in batches until golden brown, turning over once. Lift out of the oil with a slotted spoon, drain on paper towels and keep hot while frying the remainder. Garnish with parsley and serve warm.

2 large zucchini, sliced into 12 rounds

¾–1 cup all-purpose flour, seasoned with salt and pepper

¼ cup sesame seeds

2 ounces ground lamb

1 scallion, finely chopped

1 garlic clove, crushed

vegetable oil, for deep-frying

2 eggs, beaten

parsley sprigs, to garnish

Serves 4
Preparation time: 15 minutes
Cooking time: about 20 minutes

spring lamb stir-fried with garlic

1 In a bowl, mix the wine or sherry with the soy sauces and sesame oil. Add the lamb and toss to evenly coat all the slices. Cover and leave to marinate for 15 minutes.

2 Drain the lamb, reserving the marinade. Heat the vegetable oil in a wok or large frying pan. Add the meat with 2 teaspoons of marinade and fry briskly for about 2 minutes or until the meat is well browned. Add a little extra marinade, if necessary, to keep the meat from sticking.

3 Add the garlic, ginger, leek, and scallions and stir-fry for a further 3 minutes. Serve immediately.

¼ cup Chinese wine or dry sherry

¼ cup light soy sauce

2 tablespoons dark soy sauce

1 teaspoon sesame oil

12 ounces lamb fillet, thinly sliced across the grain

¼ cup vegetable oil

6 garlic cloves, thinly sliced

1-inch piece of fresh ginger, peeled and chopped

1 leek, thinly sliced diagonally

4 scallions, chopped

Serves 4

Preparation time: 5 minutes, plus marinating

Cooking time: 5–7 minutes

■ Meat is thinly sliced for stir-frying so that it is as tender as possible and cooks rapidly. It should be cut across the grain using a sharp knife or cleaver. Placing the meat in the freezer for about 1 hour before slicing makes it firm for easy cutting.

fried pork with baby corn & snow peas

1 Mix 1 teaspoon of the cornstarch to a smooth paste with the wine or sherry and soy sauce. Add the pork and toss to coat all the slices with the cornstarch paste.

2 Heat the oil in a wok or frying pan and stir-fry the pork until it is lightly browned.

3 Add the baby corn and salt, and stir-fry for 30 seconds. Add the snow peas and mushrooms, and stir-fry for 1 minute. Sprinkle the sugar over the pork mixture.

4 Mix the remaining cornstarch with the water to make a thin paste and pour this into the wok, stirring continuously. Continue to cook briefly, stirring, until the sauce is thickened. Serve immediately.

1½ teaspoons cornstarch

2 tablespoons Chinese wine or dry sherry

2 tablespoons light soy sauce

1 pound pork tenderloin, very thinly sliced

2 tablespoons sunflower oil

1 pound baby corn

1 teaspoon salt

2 ounces snow peas

15-ounce can straw mushrooms, drained

2 teaspoons sugar

2 teaspoons water

Serves 4
Preparation time: 5 minutes
Cooking time: 5–8 minutes

1 Cut the pork into small cubes and place them in a bowl. Sprinkle with the salt and brandy, then leave to marinate for 15 minutes. Add the beaten egg and cornstarch and stir well.

2 Heat the oil in a wok to 350–375°F or until a cube of day-old bread browns in 30 seconds. Meanwhile, coat the pork with flour, then fry for 3 minutes. Remove the wok from the heat, but leave the pork in the oil for 2 minutes. Use a slotted spoon to remove the pork from the oil.

3 Reheat the oil and re-fry the meat with the bamboo shoots for about 2 minutes. Remove and drain on paper towels. Carefully pour off all but 2 tablespoons of the oil. Add the scallions and green bell pepper and stir-fry for 1 minute.

4 Mix the sauce ingredients with a little juice from the canned pineapple and stir into the wok. Bring to a boil and simmer briefly until thickened. Taste and add more juice if required. Add the pork, bamboo shoots, and pineapple, mix lightly and serve hot.

8 ounces lean boneless pork

1 teaspoon salt

3 tablespoons brandy

1 egg, beaten

2 tablespoons cornstarch

vegetable oil, for deep-frying

¾ cup all-purpose flour

4 ounces canned bamboo shoots, drained and cut into small chunks

2 scallions, cut into 1-inch lengths

1 green bell pepper, cored, seeded, and cut into small chunks

15-ounce can pineapple chunks in juice

Sauce:

⅓ cup vinegar

⅓ cup sugar

½ teaspoon salt

2 tablespoons tomato paste

2 tablespoons soy sauce

2 tablespoons cornstarch

1 teaspoon sesame oil

Serves 3–4

Preparation time: 15 minutes, plus marinating

Cooking time: 15 minutes

sweet & sour pork

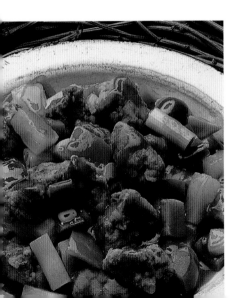

spicy pork meatballs

1 Put the pork into a bowl. Drain the crab meat in a sieve and squeeze it to remove as much liquid as possible, then add to the pork. Add half of the ginger, garlic, chilies, and cilantro with 2 tablespoons of the soy sauce. Season with salt and pepper.

2 Mix the ingredients well, using your hands, and squeeze the mixture so that it binds together. With wet hands, form the mixture into about 24 balls. Coat the meatballs in the cornstarch.

3 Heat the oil in a wok until very hot but not smoking. Cook the meatballs in batches for 2–3 minutes each, until golden and crisp all over. Remove with a slotted spoon and drain on paper towels.

4 Pour off all the oil from the wok and wipe it clean with paper towels. Return the meatballs to the wok and sprinkle with the remaining ginger, garlic, and chili. Pour in the hot stock and remaining soy sauce, sprinkle with the sugar and season to taste, then heat until simmering gently. Cover and cook gently for 15 minutes, turning the meatballs occasionally.

5 Add the Chinese cabbage, stirring it into the liquid. Simmer for 5 minutes. Serve hot, sprinkled with the remaining cilantro, the chili strips, and scallions.

8 ounces ground pork

6-ounce can white crab meat in brine

2-inch piece of fresh ginger, peeled and grated

2 garlic cloves, crushed

2 large red chilies, seeded and finely chopped

2 handfuls of cilantro leaves, roughly chopped

⅓ cup soy sauce

¼ cup cornstarch

about ¾ cup peanut oil, for frying

3 cups hot chicken stock

1 teaspoon sugar

6–7 ounces Chinese cabbage, shredded

salt and pepper

To Garnish:

1 large red chili, seeded and thinly sliced

4 scallions, shredded

Serves 4–6
Preparation time: 30 minutes
Cooking time: 35–40 minutes

stir-fried pork with eggplant

1 In a bowl, mix the pork with the scallions, ginger, garlic, soy sauce, wine or sherry, and cornstarch. Cover and leave to marinate for about 20 minutes.

2 Heat the oil for deep-frying to 350°F or until a cube of day-old bread browns in 30 seconds. Reduce the heat, add the eggplant and deep-fry for about 1½ minutes. Remove from the pan with a slotted spoon and drain on paper towels.

3 Heat 2 tablespoons of the oil from deep-frying in a wok or frying pan, then stir-fry the pork for about 1 minute. Add the eggplant and chili sauce and cook for about 1½ minutes.

4 Moisten the pork mixture with the stock or water and simmer until the liquid has almost completely evaporated. Garnish with chopped scallions and serve hot, with plain boiled rice.

6 ounces lean boneless pork, shredded

2 scallions, finely chopped

1 slice of fresh ginger, peeled and finely chopped

1 garlic clove, finely chopped

2 tablespoons soy sauce

1 teaspoon Chinese wine or dry sherry

1½ teaspoons cornstarch

vegetable oil, for deep-frying

8 ounces eggplant, cut into diamond-shaped chunks

2 tablespoons chili sauce

⅓–½ cup chicken stock or water

chopped scallion, to garnish

Serves 3–4
Preparation time: 10 minutes, plus marinating
Cooking time: 10–15 minutes

pork with bean sprouts

1 Mix the cornstarch to a smooth paste with the soy sauce, stock, sherry, and vinegar.

2 Heat the oil in a wok. Add the onion and the garlic and fry for 30 seconds. Add the pork and bean sprouts, season to taste with salt and pepper and stir-fry the mixture for a further 1 minute.

3 Pour in the cornstarch mixture, stirring, and stir-fry for a further 1½ minutes, until the juices boil and thicken. Serve immediately.

2 teaspoons cornstarch

¼ cup soy sauce

½ cup chicken stock

2 teaspoons dry sherry

¼ cup wine vinegar

⅔ cup sunflower oil

¼ cup finely chopped onion

1 garlic clove, crushed

8 ounces lean pork tenderloin, cut into thin slices

1 cup bean sprouts

salt and pepper

Serves 4
Preparation time: 10 minutes
Cooking time: 3 minutes

■ Thinly sliced beef can be used instead of pork and 4 ounces of thinly sliced mushrooms can be added to either version, with an extra 1-2 teaspoons sherry.

szechuan dry-fried shredded beef

1 Heat a wok or large frying pan over a high heat for 1 minute. Add the sesame oil and reduce the heat to moderate. Add the steak with 2 tablespoons of the wine or sherry and stir-fry to separate the shreds.

2 Reduce the heat and pour off any excess liquid, then continue to stir-fry the meat gently until it is dry. Add the chili bean paste, hoisin sauce, garlic, salt, sugar, and remaining wine or sherry. Stir-fry for 1 minute.

3 Increase the heat, add the carrots and stir-fry for 2 minutes. Add the scallions, ginger, Szechuan or black pepper, and chili oil, and stir to mix the ingredients. Serve immediately.

¼ cup sesame oil

10 ounces flank steak, cut into short fine strips

¼ cup Chinese wine or dry sherry

2 tablespoons chili bean paste

2 tablespoons hoisin sauce

1 garlic clove, finely chopped

½ teaspoon salt

2 tablespoons sugar

4 ounces carrots, cut into short fine strips

2 scallions, finely chopped

2 slices of fresh ginger, peeled and finely chopped

½ teaspoon freshly ground Szechuan or black pepper

1 teaspoon chili oil

Serves 4

Preparation time: 20 minutes

Cooking time: 15 minutes

beef with broccoli

1 In a bowl, mix together the oyster sauce, sherry, and cornstarch. Add the beef slices, turn to coat, cover, and leave to marinate in the refrigerator for about 20 minutes.

2 If using dried mushrooms, drain and squeeze dry, discard the stalks and finely slice the caps.

3 Heat half of the oil in the wok. Add the beef slices and stir-fry for 10–15 seconds. Remove with a slotted spoon and set aside.

4 Heat the remaining oil, then add the ginger and scallions, mushrooms, broccoli, bamboo shoots, and carrot. Add the salt and sugar and stir-fry for 1½ minutes. Add the beef, stir well and moisten with a little water. Heat through and serve hot.

¼ cup oyster sauce

2 tablespoons dry sherry

2 tablespoons cornflour

8 ounces steak, cut into thickish slices

4 ounces button mushrooms or 3–4 Chinese dried mushrooms, soaked in warm water for 20 minutes

½ cup vegetable oil

2 slices fresh ginger, peeled and chopped

2 scallions, chopped

6 ounces broccoli florets

4 ounces bamboo shoots, sliced

1 carrot, sliced

1 teaspoon salt

1 teaspoon sugar

Serves 4

Preparation time: 15 minutes, plus marinating

Cooking time: 5 minutes

2 tablespoons sunflower oil

1 onion, thinly sliced

1 garlic clove, crushed

12 ounces flank steak, cut into fine strips or small slices

2–3 plums, pitted and sliced

3 flat mushrooms, sliced

2 tablespoons Chinese wine or dry sherry

2 teaspoons light brown sugar

2 tablespoons dark soy sauce

2 teaspoons cornstarch

¼ cup water

2 scallions, green part only, chopped, to garnish

1 Heat the oil in a wok or large frying pan. Add the onion and fry for 2 minutes. Stir in the garlic and steak, and stir-fry over a high heat for 2 minutes.

2 Reduce the heat and add the plums and mushrooms. Continue to stir-fry for 1 minute, then stir in the wine or sherry, sugar, and soy sauce.

3 Blend the cornstarch to a smooth paste with the water add this mixture to the pan, stirring until the sauce has thickened. Garnish with chopped scallions and serve.

Serves 4
Preparation time: 6 minutes
Cooking time: 8 minutes

stir-fried beef with plum sauce & mushrooms

■ Plums add fragrant, fruity sweetness and a succulent contrast in texture to this attractive and hearty beef dish.

1 Blend the cornstarch to a smooth paste with the soy sauce in a large bowl. Add the steak and turn it in the cornstarch mixture to coat all the shreds. Cover and leave to marinate for 10 minutes.

2 Heat half of the oil in a wok or large frying pan over a high heat. Stir-fry the steak for about 1 minute or until lightly browned. Remove with a slotted spoon and set aside.

3 Heat the remaining oil in the wok and stir-fry the beans with salt to taste for 1–1½ minutes. Replace the meat and stir in the wine or sherry with a little stock or water.

4 Reheat briefly until the ingredients are combined and the steak is hot. Do not overcook the mixture— the beans should be crisp and the meat tender. Add salt to taste and serve immediately, garnished with shredded scallion.

2 tablespoons cornstarch

¼ cup light soy sauce

8 ounces flank steak, cut into short fine strips

½ cup sunflower oil

8 ounces French beans, cut into 2-inch lengths

2 tablespoons Chinese wine or dry sherry

2–4 tablespoons beef stock or water

salt

shredded scallion, to garnish

Serves 4
Preparation time: 15 minutes, plus marinating
Cooking time: 5 minutes

fried beef with french beans

stir-fried liver & spinach

1 Blanch the liver in boiling water for a few seconds. Drain well and coat with cornstarch.

2 Heat half of the oil in a wok or large frying pan. Add the spinach and the salt, and stir-fry for 2 minutes. Arrange the spinach around the edge of a warm serving dish, then set aside to keep hot.

3 Wipe the wok clean with paper towels and heat the remaining oil until very hot. Add the ginger, liver, soy sauce, and wine or sherry. Stir-fry briskly for about 1–2 minutes, taking care not to overcook the liver or it will become tough.

4 Pour the mixture into the middle of the spinach and garnish with scallion. Serve immediately.

12 ounces pig's liver, cut into thin triangular slices

¼ cup cornstarch

½ cup sunflower oil

1 pound spinach, washed and drained

1 teaspoon salt

2 thin slices of fresh ginger, peeled

2 tablespoons light soy sauce

2 tablespoons Chinese wine or dry sherry

shredded scallion, to garnish

Serves 4

Preparation time: 10 minutes

Cooking time: 3–4 minutes

stir-fried beef in hot chili sauce

1 Season the steak with salt. Heat the oil in a wok or large frying pan over a moderate heat and fry the dried red chiles for 1 minute to flavor the oil. Use a slotted spoon to remove and discard the chilies.

2 Increase the heat, then stir-fry the steak for 1 minute until all the pieces are browned.

3 Add the garlic, ginger, and scallions, and cook for 30 seconds. Stir in the soy sauces, wine or sherry, and green chilies, and cook for a further 1 minute.

4 Transfer to a warm serving dish and serve immediately.

1 pound rump steak, thinly sliced across the grain

¼ cup sunflower oil

2 dried red chilies

2 garlic cloves, sliced

1-inch piece of fresh ginger, peeled and shredded

4 scallions, shredded

¼ cup dark soy sauce

¼ cup light soy sauce

¼ cup Chinese wine or dry sherry

2 green chilies, deseeded and chopped

salt

Serves 4

Preparation time: 20 minutes

Cooking time: 4–5 minutes

■ Chinese rice wine is used in cooking, especially in sauces and marinades.

index